WHAT IF YOU HAD

Animal Scales!?

OR OTHER ANIMAL COATS?

by Sandra Markle

Illustrated by
Howard McWilliam

Scholastic Inc.

For Alana Stanton and the children of Oconee County Primary School in Watkinsville, Georgia.

A special thank-you to Skip Jeffery for his loving support during the creative process.

The author would like to thank the following people for sharing their enthusiasm and expertise: Dr. Timothy J. Colston, Florida State University, Tallahassee, Florida (African Bush Viper); Dr. Gareth J. Fraser, University of Florida, Gainesville, Florida (Hammerhead Shark); Dr. Angela B. Keffer, Robinson Animal Hospital, Mckees Rocks, Pennsylvania (Chinchilla); Dr. Gerald Kooyman, Research Professor Emeritus, Scripps Institution of Oceanography, University of California-San Diego, La Jolla, California (Emperor Penguin); Dr. Tom McCarthy, Panthera, New York, New York (Leopard); Dr. Eric Pianka, University of Texas, Austin, Texas (Thorny Devil); Dr. Simon Pollard, University of Canterbury, Christchurch, New Zealand (Honeybee and Tarantula); Dr. George Olah, Australian National University, Canberra, Australia (Scarlet Macaw); Dr. Ewan St. John Smith, University of Cambridge, Cambridge, UK (Naked Mole Rat); Dr. Julian Vincent, Heriot-Watt University, Edinburgh, Scotland (European Hedgehog)

Photos ©: cover wood sign and throughout: Dim Dimich/Shutterstock; cover bottom right: Joe McDonald/Getty Images; cover background: kdshutterman/Shutterstock; 4: Damian Duffy/Shutterstock; 4 inset: WorldFoto/Alamy Stock Photo; 6: Savushkin/Getty Images; 6 inset: Nature Picture Library/Alamy Stock Photo; 8: by wildestanimal/Getty Images; 8 inset: Ted Kinsman/Science Source; 10: Norayr Avagyan/Getty Images; 10 inset: Fernando Trabanco Fotografía/Getty Images; 12: Sylvain Cordier/NPL/Minden Pictures; 12 inset: Nature Picture Library/Alamy Stock Photo; 14: Neil Bromhall/Shutterstock; 14 inset: Frans Lanting/National Geographic Image Collection; 16: Joe McDonald/Getty Images; 16 inset: Mark_Kostich/Shutterstock; 18: Artur Rydzewski/Alamy Stock Photo; 18 inset: John Kimbler/National Geographic Image Collection; 20: VW Pics/Getty Images; 20 inset: stockphoto mania/Shutterstock; 22: Aditya Singh/Getty Images; 22 inset: Kris Wiktor/Shutterstock; 24: Milan Zygmunt/Shutterstock; 24 inset: FLPA/Alamy

Library of Congress Cataloging-in-Publication Data available

ISBN 978-1-338-66614-4

10 9 8 7 6 5   22 23 24 25

Printed in the U.S.A.   40
First edition, November 2021

Book design by Kay Petronio

What if one day when you woke up, you felt a little bit strange? And you discovered that, overnight, the skin covering your body was now VERY different? What if a wild animal's scales or some other animal coat had taken its place?

THORNY DEVIL

The thorny devil's scaly coat has thin channels of bare skin running between spiky scales. These channels collect rainwater and soak up water from wet sand or humid air. By opening and closing its mouth, the thorny devil pulls a drink from its channel network. GULP! GULP!

FACT

A thorny devil's coat is too spiky for most predators to bite.

If you had a thorny devil's coat, you'd enjoy being caught in the rain.

CHINCHILLA

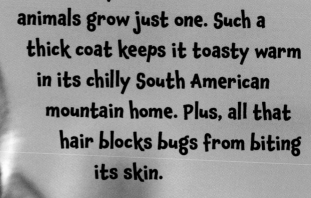

The chinchilla holds the record for thickest fur of any land animal. Each hair-growing spot on its skin sprouts fifty hairs where most animals grow just one. Such a thick coat keeps it toasty warm in its chilly South American mountain home. Plus, all that hair blocks bugs from biting its skin.

FACT

A chinchilla baby, called a kit, is born with its eyes open and a full coat of fur.

If you had
chinchilla fur,
you'd never need
bug spray.

HAMMERHEAD SHARK

A hammerhead shark cruises at 15 miles per hour—and can reach even faster speeds for short bursts. The secret is its coat of denticles. These are hard, overlapping, toothlike scales so tiny that about 10,000 of them cover a patch of the shark's skin no bigger than a U.S. penny. Together, denticles create a coat of armor that water easily slips past, letting the shark zip through the ocean. No wonder a hammerhead shark can dine on fast food, such as sardines!

FACT

A hammerhead's denticles grow out of its skin—the way hairs and feathers do—but each one is like a tiny tooth, with a soft inner pulp and hard enamel cover.

If you had a hammerhead shark's coat of denticles, you'd shock everyone by how fast you can swim!

EUROPEAN HEDGEHOG

A European hedgehog's coat is prickly, with spines sticking out of its back and sides. Each spine is a tube made of keratin—the same strong stuff your fingernails are made of—and has a honeycomb filling. That makes the hedgehog's spiny coat a natural shock absorber. Its spines are flexible enough to bend without breaking and stiff enough to straighten again. No wonder, if a European hedgehog falls, it balls up and twists to land on its shock-absorbing back. Sometimes it even bounces!

FACT

As a European hedgehog grows up, its baby spines fall out—one by one—and are replaced by longer, adult spines.

If you had a European hedgehog's coat, you'd bounce and safely perform amazing jump rope stunts.

EMPEROR PENGUIN

An emperor penguin's feathers help it survive in Antarctica, the coldest place on Earth. Stiff outer feathers overlap for a tough, waterproof cover. Beneath this, lots of fluffy feathers form super-thick insulating underwear. Together these layers are the perfect coat for staying warm, sliding on ice, and swimming in ice-cold water.

FACT

An emperor penguin sheds and replaces its feather coat yearly. While that's happening, it stays on land for about a month without eating.

If you had an emperor penguin's coat, you'd be a champion water slide racer.

NAKED MOLE RAT

A naked mole rat isn't completely naked. It has fine hairs—mainly in rows down the sides of its body. These are important sensors that help it find its way through the dark underground tunnels of its colony's home. Thanks to these hairs, it navigates without running into tunnel walls or accidentally bumping into other naked mole rats.

FACT

A naked mole rat has hairs filling the spaces between its toes. These hairs help it push dirt while digging new tunnels.

If you had a naked mole rat's coat, you'd lead expeditions into deep, unexplored places.

AFRICAN BUSH VIPER

An African bush viper's scaly coat acts as body armor when crawling on trees and bushes. Muscles move its belly scales to power it forward. The scale edges press against rough spots, anchoring its grip. When the snake stays still, its ridged scales help it mimic leaves or fruit to hide from big, hungry birds. If a small bird or lizard comes close, it strikes. Dinnertime!

FACT

An African bush viper sheds the outer layer of its skin a few times a year, as all snakes do. It's how it grows bigger and freshens its scaly armor.

If you had an African bush viper's scaly coat, you wouldn't need steps to reach your tree house.

HONEYBEE

A honeybee's body is covered with nearly three million hairs. Pollen sticks to these hairs when the bee lands on a flower to sip nectar. By brushing and licking, the bee cleans its body, pushing the pollen onto its hind legs. There, a fringe of extra-long hairs act like pollen saddlebags. When they are packed full, the bee flies this food home to its hive and colony.

FACT

Even a honeybee's eyes are hairy. Scientists believe these hairs detect wind direction. That may help the bee stay on course while flying from flowers to its hive on windy days.

If you had a honeybee's coat, you'd always have the biggest haul on Halloween.

SCARLET MACAW

A scarlet macaw's feather coat can't be missed. But showing off in its forest home is a good thing. Predators, such as eagles and jaguars, know not to mess with the bright, big bird with the strong, ready-to-bite beak. Colorful, shiny feathers also show good health, which scientists believe scarlet macaws look for when choosing their lifelong mates.

FACT

Scarlet macaw pairs share preening—running their beaks through each other's feathers to clean and smooth them.

If you had a scarlet macaw's coat, you'd start a wild-colored hair fad.

LEOPARD

A leopard's coat makes it a super-sneaky cat. Its coloring lets it blend into patches of sunlight and shadow in Africa's grasslands. The spotted pattern makes the leopard's body shape hard to see. So although it runs slower than a cheetah, a leopard's coat lets it sneak close enough to catch fast food, such as antelope.

FACT

Like your fingerprints are unique to you, each leopard is born with its own one-of-a-kind coat pattern.

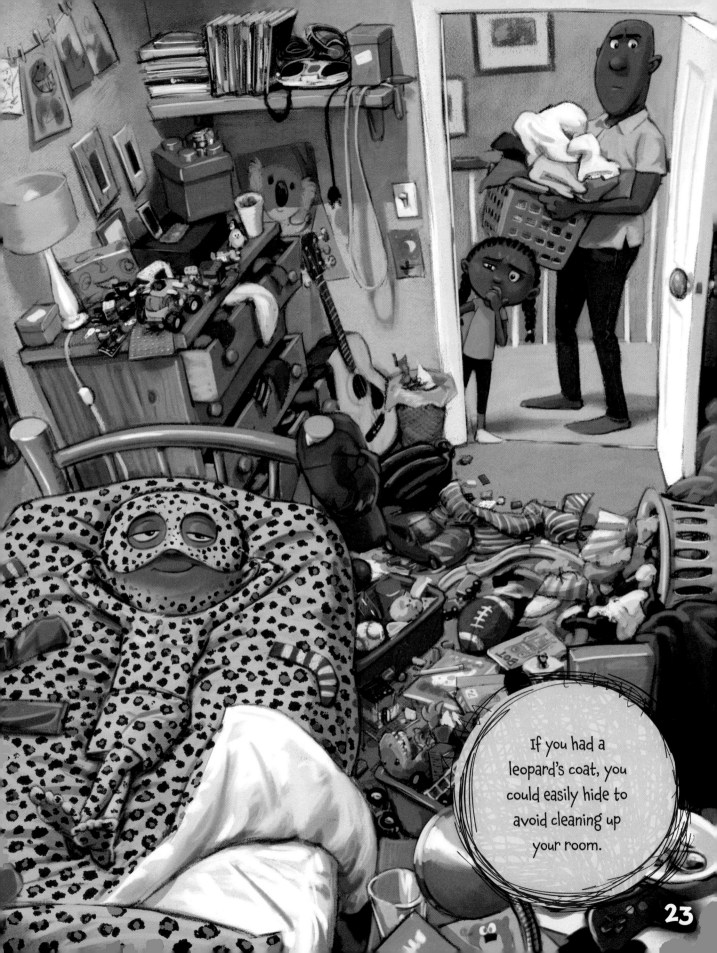

If you had a leopard's coat, you could easily hide to avoid cleaning up your room.

GOLIATH BIRDEATER
TARANTULA

A goliath birdeater tarantula's dinner plate–sized body has a shell-like covering with a very hairy coat. It doesn't hear, smell, or see well, so its hairs are how the tarantula senses what's around it. Special hairs near its feet give it a sense of taste so it knows if what it touches is dinner.

FACT

If threatened, a goliath birdeater tarantula rubs its back legs across its abdomen, flicking off a stinging cloud of barb-tipped hairs.

If you had a goliath birdeater tarantula's coat, you'd be a world-famous restaurant critic.

Having a wild animal's coat could be cool for a while, but you don't need a new body covering to bounce, get a drink, or go exploring. Plus, you can stand out

in a crowd just the way you are. So, if you could keep an animal's scales or another wild coat for more than a day, which kind would be right for you?

Luckily, you don't have to choose. The covering on your body will always be human skin. It's what you need to keep your body fluids inside and keep out germs—tiny living things that can make you sick. It's also what keeps you

from getting too warm or too cold. Plus, your skin helps you feel pain.
Pain is important because it lets you know to take action to stay safe.
Best of all, your skin is what you need to look like you!

WHAT'S SPECIAL ABOUT YOUR SKIN?

Your skin is made up of three layers: the epidermis, the dermis, and the subcutaneous fat. These work together to keep your body healthy.

Epidermis

This layer is the part of your skin you can see. It protects your insides and holds you together. It's thin in some places, such as your eyelids, and thick in other places, such as the soles of your feet. This layer also contains melanin, the material that gives your skin your exactly-you color.

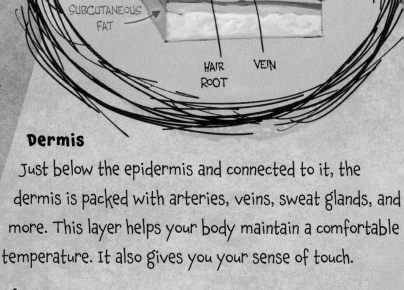

EPIDERMIS

SWEAT GLAND

DERMIS

SUBCUTANEOUS FAT

ARTERY

HAIR ROOT

VEIN

Dermis

Just below the epidermis and connected to it, the dermis is packed with arteries, veins, sweat glands, and more. This layer helps your body maintain a comfortable temperature. It also gives you your sense of touch.

Subcutaneous Fat

Because it is mostly fat, this layer helps insulate your body s you stay warm. And it's a shock absorber to help cushion your insides against a hard bump or fall.

KEEP YOUR SKIN HEALTHY

Your skin needs to be in good condition for you to be healthy. Here are some tips for taking care of your skin.

- Wash regularly with soap and water. Then gently pat dry.

- Be careful when doing anything that might cut or scrape your skin, such as playing a sport.

- Be super careful around anything that could burn your skin, such as a tray of cookies coming out of a hot oven.

- Cover up with sunscreen and clothing to shield your skin from the sun.

- Cover your skin as much as possible when walking through tall grass or in the woods to help shield yourself from insect bites.

OTHER BOOKS IN THE SERIES

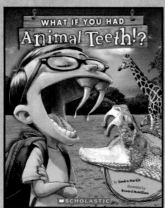

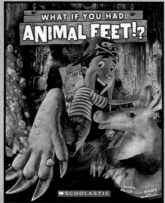

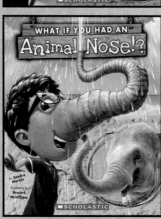

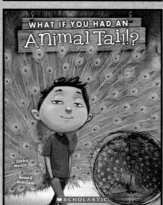

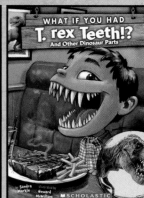

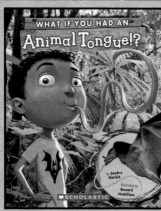

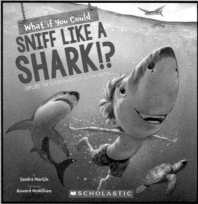

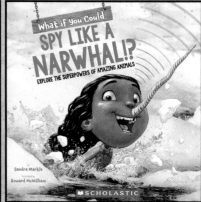